But We Get Up...

Bouncing Back After Life's Knockdowns

by

A.T. Wright

Table of Contents

Prologue

"Land of the Free, Home of the Brave!" This phrase penned by Francis Scott Key in 1814 was originally crafted as a poem later becoming the lyrics for The Star Spangled Banner, the National Anthem of the United States of America. A quick Google search of Francis Scott Key and you will discover that he was a lawyer, writer, and a former United States District Attorney. Delve a little deeper, and you may be astounded to find that he was also a former slave owner who frequently referred to blacks as "a distinct and inferior race of people." We could go on about Mr. Key, but I will spare the readers the history lesson. Nevertheless, I do want to analyze the grammatical construction of the phrase "Land of the Free, Home of the Brave." The phrase itself appears to be very contradictory to say the least!

It is common knowledge that the United States was founded and built mainly by Europeans through centuries of the enslavement and oppression of other peoples, namely Native Americans and Black Africans. Due to the abolishment of slavery in 1865, the United States was forced to find another source of free labor. In response, the powers that be developed what is now known as the United States prison system.

Currently, the U.S makes up about five percent of the world's population, and twenty-five percent of the worlds incarcerated population. As of July 2018, for every one-hundred thousand people living in the United States, six hundred and fifty-five individuals are behind bars. This number is by far the highest of any nation in the world! To put these staggering statistics into perspective, the U.S houses more inmates than the top thirty-five European countries combined! According to the Bureau of Prison Statistics, as of November of 2018, demographically African Americans make up just thirteen percent of the U.S population however they account for thirty-eight percent of the prison population!" Land of the Free, Home of the Brave?" Perhaps a more appropriately bestowed phrase would be "Land of the Free, Home of the Imprisoned."

Now, this is, after all, a motivational book, so at this point, you may be questioning the relevance of these depressing prison statistics. The relevance lies in the reality that at twenty-two years of age I found myself ensnared in the net of that "system." I was a former standout high school athlete and a recent college drop out with no prior criminal record. I had never even experienced trouble with the law as a juvenile. The relative quantity of my adolescent years was spent with a basketball in my hands or practicing some other form of athletics. But there I found myself, first offense resulting in six years in state prison on a felony one aggravated robbery charge. I was soon shipped off to serve my time at Toledo Correctional Institution, a close security prison three hours away from home.

I spent six years in the state prison working my way down from that close security prison to minimum security at Belmont Correctional Institution. I also spent that time formulating my plan for the day when I would reclaim my freedom and repossess my life! To say it was the longest of journeys would be an understatement! Confined behind those concrete walls and barbwire fences, I was forced to navigate my way through power crazed correctional officers and inmates that represented every spectrum in the rainbow of criminality. The living conditions included being stacked in a warehouse type dorm housing seven hundred inmates but build to hold five-hundred! No air conditioning, imagine that in the summertime! Mentally, I battled through bouts of depression, panic, guilt, anger and abandonment issues. People assume that the physical aspects of being imprisoned are what's hardest to deal with. I'm here to tell you that the physical has nothing on the mental perspective. If you are not of the strong mind, there is a great chance that you will leave that place with mental health issues!

As harsh as the environment of life behind those cold concrete walls may have been, the true test of a man once he loses his freedom is dealing with the outside occurrences of the world. While you are locked inside, your family and friends are on the outside dealing with real-life challenges that you are powerless to help with impact.

I recall several of the major occurrences that transpired outside of those walls that challenged not only my faith but my overall sanity! One of those instance was calling my son's mother to get an update on her and my son. In the background I could hear my son and clear as day, I heard him call someone Dad! Not only did she inform me that yes my son calls her boyfriend Dad, but she was also getting married. Talk about a slap in the face! Another of those challenging times was the day I called home only to be informed that my mother was just rushed to the hospital from an apparent heart attack, which turned into triple bypass surgery. Just when I thought things couldn't possibly get any worse, I received news that there was a serious car accident involving my mother, my son and my son's mother! Finding myself at my rock bottom, I began to feel overwhelmed with being powerless. The powerless feeling only served to intensify the impression that every painful occurrence that transpired on the outside of those walls, in one way or another was my fault. Each time occurrences like these happened I piled more guilt upon my plate.

Three and a half years into my incarceration I was convinced that my time had come to go home. Immediately following the expiration of the mandatory portion of my sentence, I filed for Judicial Release, which in Ohio is a form of parole. I had many factors working in my favor. Not only was it my first offense, but I also had, for the most part, stayed out of trouble for the entirety of my sentence. I also completed Barber College and was now a licensed Master Barber! I figured I was a lock to receive Judicial Release! Usually, a lawyer on the outside would handle motions such as these. But because no one on the outside had the seven hundred dollars to pay the lawyer to file the paperwork, that wasn't an option for me.

Instead, I spent hours in the law library learning the law and eventually filed the motion myself. Finally, I submitted the motion. I sent it in on a Friday and judging by how long my mail takes to get to my family; I estimated that the motion would be received by the courts by Wednesday of the next week. Being aware of the process, I calculated that it would take at least a month for the courts to get the motion for Judicial Release and make a determination. To my amazement, I received a reply via the courts Friday of the next week! This was exactly seven days after I sent the motion in... Denied! I still don't know how it was possible for the mail to move that fast! It seemed like they already had their denial papers stamped and ready to send just for when I filed! My response was to attend programs such as A.A and N.A to show that I had taken advantage of my time. I also became a volunteer tutor for the GED program. Once again I filed the motion and once again I was denied! I would go on to file early release paperwork three times only to be denied each time!

Despite all the factors that were in my favor to be released early, I ended up doing every last day of that sentence! Never did get that early release, rare for someone with no prior record.

Are you depressed enough yet? Don't worry, though I will share my experiences, this is not a memoir about me doing time. This is not a story about unjust prison sentences in the African American community, nor the "business "of prison that many of our brothers and sisters fall victim to. (That's the next book) This is my story about how I used my own personal "rock bottom" as the launching pad for my comeback. But We Get Up...Bouncing Back After Life's Knockdowns is a guide to how I leveraged the most trying obstacle of my life and came back stronger, determined and more focused than ever before!

Throughout my journey, I've acquired valuable tools that have aided me in being able to get up off the canvas after life delivered a punishing blow. I credit those tools with not only getting me back up on my feet but also allowing me to realize my potential and flourish! My goal is to share those tools with you to help you make it on your comeback journey. By sharing my experiences, I hope to inspire you the reader into realizing that you also can use potential setbacks to set up your future.

When I walked out of Belmont Correctional Institution a little over a decade ago, it was a foregone conclusion that I was facing an uphill climb. When I initially made my re-entry into society, my life possessions included ten dollars, a sweat suit and a pair of sneakers! Not counting my mother's one-bedroom apartment that of course, I was welcome to, I was homeless. I had no driver's license, no car, no money, no job, no clothes, no health insurance. I had to pull myself up from my bootstraps and start from scratch. But more important than everything I lacked, I had a plan! I also had an unwavering belief in myself that bordered on arrogance for someone in my position! I took all of that pain, torment, embarrassment, and suffering and used it to light a fire of motivation in my soul that has only burned brighter with each passing day! I had been to the proverbial "rock- bottom." I had fought for my life and my sanity! I was determined, and I knew that no matter what came my way it could not compare to the six years of my life that I had lost. I was determined to make those six years count!

Today, that drive and determination have lead me to be the first member of my family to graduate from college. That impetus has also lead me to be the owner of two businesses and the Founder/CEO of a Non-Profit Organization. I took advantage of the barber license I received during my incarceration and parlayed it into eventually owning my barbershop. That drive has not only pushed me to complete and publish But We Get Up, it has also motivated me to incorporate my own publishing company Our Voices Publishing, giving others the opportunity to have their stories heard as well.

In 2016 I founded The Young Scholars Mentoring Center Inc., a 501(c)(3) non-profit organization where our mission is to prevent at-risk youth from falling into life's pitfalls that many of them face on a daily basis. By providing youth with the tools for success, Y.S.M.C has been able to positively effect change in the youth we come into contact with. Outside of our mentoring and tutoring services, we also have been successful in employing an ever-expanding staff. In addition, we have been able to provide college scholarships while also orchestrating numerous food, clothing, and school drives. Each day we gain more momentum and grow as a business and an asset to the community at large.

I've also begun to spread my story as a motivational speaker at some of the same prisons in which I served my six-year sentence. Imagine that! There is no way I could ever explain the feeling of walking back through those gates as a guest. It is nearly an out of body experience every time! I know there are a lot of rewards in life, money, vacations, children, and family. But to have someone shake your hand, look you in the eyes and thank you for being an inspiration to them, for me it doesn't get much better.

People look at me and admire how far I've come and the direction my life is headed. They consider me a role model and an asset to my community. But I feel like I'm just getting started and I am far from being satisfied. I have dreams and goals that I have yet to realize. I still have struggles that I must face and correct to truly find my ultimate happiness. I want to further my education and receive a master's degree! I'm still single; I'd love to find and marry my queen! I can admit that focusing on business has taken away from a lot of time that I should have been spending with my son. I don't do and say all the right things. I still have my trials and tribulations that I must overcome on a daily basis. However, having the courage of full transparency and the ability to accept the worse things about yourself and work to fix them, that's how you win!

But We Get Up...Bouncing Back After Life's Knockdowns is for anyone who has suffered adversity, setback, heartbreak or disappointment. It is for anyone who feels like life has delivered its most lethal punch and knocked you down! Not only can you pick yourself up off the canvas of life but you can also punch back and win! Today is the day you reclaim your life!

Chapter 1

Take Responsibility to Avoid Being a Victim

I'm here as proof that life is not always going to be beautiful! In fact, for a lot of us, life is going to be a twelve round, knockdown, drag-out fight! Prepare yourself, my friends, during that fight life is going to deliver blows from every angle imaginable! Uppercuts, hooks, and jabs will be pummeled down upon us in the form of heartbreaking tragedies, financial problems, failed relationships, medical issues and in extreme cases even the loss of our freedom. Characteristics such as race, gender, financial standing, and education level provide no defense as no one is immune from the barrage of punches life can deliver.

For a vast majority of us, those punches can cause us to back into a corner and become stuck in the mindset of "I don't deserve this, why me?" I was no different. Many a night I lay in the dark on that cold steel bunk not able to concentrate on anything except how I had been made a victim. During those nights alone with my thoughts, I spent a lot of time questioning God on how He could let this happen to me. I blamed Him! When the buzz of fluorescent lights would awaken me from my sleep at four am, I would begin my daily routine of placing the blame on more worldly targets. The majority of my conversations centered around the rationalization of how the "system" is corrupt and used as a means to lock young African American men like me behind bars. I would continually recapitulate a scenario where my lawyer had "sacrificed me" in a deal with the prosecutor, implying that they were operating on a quid pro quo basis (favor for a favor). Now, are these valid issues that occur within the criminal justice system? Absolutely! Are there deals being made behind the scenes prematurely securing the outcomes of potential convictions? I'm convinced! Is it true that judges and prosecutors will push extra hard for convictions during election time as a means to increase voter popularity? Without a doubt! The more I communicated these stories to the people around me, the more I was able to convince myself that they were true and happened to me. But behind the facade of elaborately constructed excuses relevant or not, what I was doing was throwing myself the biggest pity party I could come up with! "Woe is me, how could this happen to me, it's their fault!"

We all know someone like this. Every event that transpires in their lives of a negative nature is more often than not someone else's fault. Nothing in their lives ever improves because they never take the necessary steps to alter their actions or thinking! These types of people accept their defeats and find comfort in their self-pity. They refuse to get up after that knockdown and take responsibility for their life, their career, their relationships, and their finances. They explain away or reason why their actions or lack of did not affect the situation or the outcome. You will find these people in the same places, telling the same stories, doing the same things waiting for change to miraculously come. Their favorite saying is "it's not my fault." They embrace being the victim! At one point in my life, that person described me perfectly.

There are several explanations as to why people embrace the victim role. One of those explanations lies in the fact that as long as you are the victim, you can internally justify feeling sorry for yourself. The longer you believe that those feelings are justified, the longer you can continue without taking responsibility for your actions or lack thereof. These people believe that as long as they are the victim, others should take the responsibility of reimbursing them of life's setbacks. However, that's not how it works! There is no celestial being or human being for that matter, who is going to magically appear to make sure we are all dealt a fair hand or reimburse us of our losses.

Another reason people embrace the victim role is often in an attempt to garner the attention they otherwise feel they do not receive. For these "poor, unfortunate'" folks, playing the victim card is an attempt at receiving empathy from individuals they come into contact with. Scroll your social media timelines, day in and day out you will see these people with new issues that require every one of their followers to pray for them. Every negative issue they are subjected to will soon be made public for all to see and know about. They are constantly voluntarily offering commentary on some injustice done to them or how others are denying them what they need, want or deserve. These people will not only seek attention for their hardships; they will seek attention by taking ownership of others hardships as well. The attention they get makes them feel better about themselves, boosts their self-esteem, and it doesn't matter if that attention is good or bad.

Lastly, the victim mentality is often used as an internal act of defiance. Eventually, this kind of victim realizes that they are no longer receiving the attention they were seeking or that they no longer can internally justify feeling sorry for themselves. In response, they assume that something will change if they dig in and yell at the top of their lungs to remind the universe that they deserve better.

But there is always an underlying price to pay for being the victim. That price is paid in relinquishing your power.

We have all heard the famous quote about how the ultimate measure of a person is where they stand in times of challenge and controversy. At numerous times in our lives, we are all going to experience negative moments due to our actions and to factors that are not in our control. Understand, it is not those moments that define us; it's our choices and reactions after those moments that make us who we are! In those moments lie golden opportunities for us to mature as human beings that can only be realized when we learn to stop being the victim and make a choice to take responsibility for our lives.

To rid yourself of the victim mentality, you need to be able to alter your victim perceptions and prohibit yourself from indulging in thoughts of self-pity. My breakthrough arrived when I finally reclaimed the responsibility of making my life what I wanted it to be. Instead of blaming everyone else, I turned the finger of responsibility towards myself. Not the finger of blame, the finger of responsibility! I examined myself internally and took responsibility for where I was at that particular time in my life. I realized that everything I did was based on the choices that I made. I took that responsibility, and I embraced it!

Correspondent to discipline, responsibility is one of those words in the English language that you have likely been bombarded with by authority figures for most of your life. Just hearing the word can cause some of us to roll our eyes in disgust remembering mom or dad drilling home the importance of taking responsibility. Still, taking responsibility is unequivocally the most important tools in acquiring the ability to grow and to feel great about yourself and your life. Without taking responsibility as the foundation for your comeback, nothing you read here or receive from other motivational platforms will work.

First, one must understand the concept of taking responsibility. Personally, when I took responsibility, I was not making an admission of guilt for the crime I had been convicted of. I was not even proclaiming that it was my fault! Me taking responsibility was me taking my power back! As long as I was placing the blame on outside forces and stuck in the mindset of whose fault it was, I remained stuck in that victim mentality. Behind all of that talking and running around pointing the finger at everything and everyone besides myself, I was the one who was suffering! I gave all the outside forces the power over my feelings, thoughts, and life by making them responsible for my life. Taking responsibility meant that I would offer no more excuses, no denial. I would take control of my life back!

What taking responsibility is not is a magic pill that you can swallow and suddenly everything in your life begins to come together. It doesn't mean that all of a sudden you don't feel the pain and that it does not affect your feelings or mood. It doesn't mean that you agree with what has transpired or that you won't fight to rectify the situation if you are wronged. I admit that almost twenty years later, I would still like to have a conversation in a room with my lawyer, judge, and prosecutor! But only when I took responsibility was I able to address the issues within myself that put my freedom in their hands in the first place. From that point forward my attitude starting changing and I started having positive thoughts. That is when I started to be able to think clearly and figure out where I went wrong and how to not only fix it but make sure it never happened again! That is when I was able to get back to looking forward to living life knowing that never again would I relinquish my power!

Another positive effect of taking responsibility is that you become honest with yourself. At times we need to take a step back and look at the entirety of our lives. Once I did this I realized that along my path there were many opportunities for me to avoid ever being locked behind those bars. I made a choice not to take advantage of the opportunity to attend college; I didn't study and get the grades. Instead, I chose to drink, smoke marijuana and party. How different would my life have been as a twenty-two-year-old college graduate? Once I flunked out of college, I chose to put myself in negative situations and surround myself with negative influences. I chose not to wake up and go to work but instead to be in the streets hustling backward. I had people around me telling me the right things to do, people who were positive examples, I ignored all those people. I looked at the lack of support I was receiving from the outside during my incarceration. A result of how I treated people, how I took advantage of relationships. How I pushed the people, who cared for me away. Those were all my choices, and I was living the results of those choices.

Ultimately for myself, taking responsibility ignited a hunger in me that pushes me every day of my life to accomplish my goals and dreams — believing that I am truly responsible for my life and what I want out of it gives me the drive to get up at six in the morning and keep working late at night when others are sleeping. Taking one hundred percent responsibility for my actions, my thoughts, and my goals have allowed me to free up the mental space formerly inhabited by negativity. The embarrassment I felt has been transformed into something positive, and that is the ability to relate and sympathize with people who are going through some of life's hardest battles. Taking responsibility has allowed me to be mindful of how I treat others and has improved all of my relationships with the people around me and those I come into contact with. Taking responsibility has allowed me to remove the roadblocks to success and set me free to focus on succeeding!

Wherever you are reading this please, just take a moment and savor the possibility that you can truly make your life whatever you want it to be! If there are hardships that you have endured, make the decision right now to move forward using those situations as fuel to power your comeback! If you want to bounce back financially, take the responsibility of letting your actions create those opportunities! Go back to school, get a trade, start a business! If there are people in your circle, who do not appreciate you, respect you or treat you how you should be treated, take the responsibility of removing those people from your life! "I am the master of my destiny," its sounds rather corny to say out loud but internally that is the power you unlock when you take responsibility for your life.

Now, you've taken a brutal right hand from your opponent called life, and you were down for the count. Symbolically, taking responsibility for that knockdown, and removing your victim mentality gets you up off the canvas and back up on one knee. At this point you're hurt, you're angry, and you're disappointed for getting knocked down. Embrace those feelings because these are the moments in which your life begins to change. In taking responsibility, you have earned your most important tool to power you on your comeback journey. The next time life throws that haymaker you'll not only see it coming, but you'll be prepared with your counter punch! In this journey of life keep in mind, responsibility isn't given, it's taken!

> *"None of us are responsible for all the things that happen to us, but we are responsible for the way we act when they do happen."*

.

Chapter Two

Power of Your Reason

Consider the times in your life when you were facing a significant crisis. Reflect on the times when you believed that things were the worse they could ever possibly be. Can you recall those times when you felt like you wouldn't make it through or that you couldn't possibly go on? If you're reading this book, you made it through those moments! Without even realizing it you were able to dig deep into the core of your being where there is a reservoir of strength, courage, and determination. No doctor or scientist has ever been able to pinpoint the origin of these reserves. However, every human being has those reserves inside of them that provide them with those remarkable abilities.

We have all been awed by stories of people who have succeeded in their lives despite the odds or horrific conditions they have suffered. We have been amazed by people who have appeared to miraculously recover from what seemed to be a life-threatening injuries or diseases. You've also heard stories of people that have lost entire families to terrible tragedies and moved on to find happiness in their lives. What about the numerous stories of down on their luck, homeless individuals who have bounced back to become multimillionaire business owners? What made these stories possible? How were these extraordinary people able to take those knockdowns and bounce back? Those people were able to tap into that supernatural power which all of us can unlock. The power of a clear and precise reason!

To put it into perspective, the power of a reason is comparable to the very light that hits our faces when we walk out of the door every day. For most of us, that light is harmless, and we can conduct our lives barely even noticing it. However, if we were to focus that same light through a magnifying glass, it becomes capable of burning and even setting things on fire! If you concentrate that light, even more, it becomes a powerful laser beam capable of carving its way through the thickest of metals! Likewise, the power of a reason enables you to focus your efforts on what matters most compelling you to push forward regardless of whatever obstacles lie in your path! The power of your reason will enable you to absorb life's hardest punches like the prize fighter you are destined to be! Having a reason empowers you to get up, to fight back and to never quit, making you capable of accomplishing anything!

At the beginning of my prison sentence, I could not get over the fact that I would be almost thirty years old when I reclaimed my freedom! I know, thirty is still relatively young but try explaining that to someone in their early twenties! However, it was not the fact that I would be pushing thirty upon my release that I couldn't wrap my mind around. It was the fact that I had to do six years! Anyway, I broke it down it still seemed like a lifetime. Trust me; I did that math many times! Two thousand one hundred and ninety days. Fifty-two thousand five hundred and sixty hours. Frequently, I would look at the calendar and say to myself "man, I'm never getting out of here!" Those years seemed like a lifetime, and it was never easy.

At some point early on I began to experience these strange recurring dizzy spells accompanied by chest pain, loss of breath, sweat and several times even vomiting. They came when I was walking, sitting, working out or in the shower. I could be just watching TV, or I could be playing ping pong, it didn't matter, they would hit anytime, anywhere. These "episodes" would last for about ten seconds then be gone, and I'd be back to normal. I know, ten seconds doesn't sound like a considerable amount of time. But trust me, it's one thing to hold your breath for ten seconds, it's an entirely different feeling when you're trying to breath for ten seconds and you can't! I began to get worried as the frequency of these attacks escalated. Honestly, with the history of heart disease in my family, I was convinced that I had minor heart attacks and that I was leading up to a big one! Don't laugh, at the time "minor heart attacks" sounded realistic to me! You couldn't tell me that I wasn't on my way to the upper room to see Elizabeth like an episode off of Sanford and Son!

Eventually, I put in an emergency notice to the doctor. Imagine the look on their faces when I told them I'd had small heart attacks and that they needed to take action before I had "the big one!" Surprisingly, they sprang into action! After several expensive tests including a few electrocardiograms, I came to find out what I was experiencing was frequent panic attacks. My worrying was putting so much stress on myself that it was effecting me mentally and now literally making me physically sick!

The doctor, an older woman in her mid to late fifties, asked me how much time I had. I told her two thousand one hundred and nineteen days! Her response would go on to have a huge impact on the direction of my life from that point on. For the first time since I had been in her office, she looked me directly in my eyes. She said "look you are here now. You know how much time you have and you know what you have to do. Find a reason to keep pushing forward and focus on what you're going to do next." She was right! I had to move away from the stress I was putting on myself, and instead of focusing on those six years, I had to start focusing on the fact that I did not get life and I would be getting out...eventually. How could I not?

Six days before turning myself in for sentencing, my first and only child was born! Andrew Zamir, affectionately known as Little Drew. It was a blessing that I was able to remain free on bond just long enough to be there when he came into the world. All I can say is God knows me best! He knew that I was going to need the motivation to make it through the next several years. By allowing me to be there to see my son being born, He provided that. As I sat in the doctor's office that day, I thought of my son. He became my reason! He became my reason to take responsibility and move forward. He was my reason to stop playing the victim role. He became the reason for me to be a better man and to set better examples. He was the reason I had to get myself together before I ended up being a frequent flier on the trip to 7:30 pill call. (7:30 is the time in prison when inmates line up to receive their anti-depressive/anti-psychotic pills).

I returned to the confines of my cell and started watching my son grow up in my mind. I started imagining the little league games, the kindergarten graduations, learning to ride a bike, learning to swim. I thought about him growing up and talking to his friends about me, telling them what I do and how cool of a dad I am. I thought about how I could end the cycle of physical abuse that had plagued our family for generations. I thought about him being a young black man in the United States. I thought about where I was and how I never wanted him to be sitting in my situation. I sat, and I envisioned his whole life and included me in it. That became my reason! I thought about my mother, my nieces, and my siblings, they became my reason! My reason became the fact that I wanted to be the best I could be for them! My reason became internal! I became self-driven! This marked the point in my life that I no longer needed to be rewarded or motivated by monetary things. This was the moment that I decided that I was not going to be a victim, I had too much to fight for!

One of my least favorite questions that I am often forced to answer is "What made you start The Young Scholars Mentoring Center?" I wish I could answer that simple question with a nice cheery "I wanted to give back to my community, help the kids where I grew up at, share my experiences." However, the truth is that the motivation behind The Young Scholars Mentoring Center is a young man by the name of Paris Wicks II.

Once I was released from prison, I began working at First Class Cuts, a local barbershop in Akron, Ohio. I first met Paris when he was an eighth-grader as he became one of my barbershop regulars. He was already an outstanding football player but what I liked about him was his humble, quiet demeanor. He reminded me of, well he reminded me of myself. As the years went past, I got to know him very well as he was in the shop every Saturday. I watched Paris grow up before my eyes and by the time he was a senior in high school he had become one of the best football players in the state of Ohio! Tightening our connection, he chose to attend Youngstown State University, the same college I attended out of high school! Tragically, on a weekend trip home from college, Paris was gunned down at a convenience store during a fight between his friend and another young man. At that point in my life, I had been to dozens of funerals but never of anyone that young, someone who had so much of his life ahead of him. This became a life-changing moment for me.

There is no doubt that his death was very hard to understand. When a senseless tragedy like that happens, it is easy to be angry, hurt and depressed. I had to check myself! I had to realize that what I was feeling was nothing compared to what his family was feeling. I had to gather myself and use the tools I had acquired that helped me recover from the worse period of my own life. I applied those same tools in response to being punched in the mouth on this occasion, instead of backing into that corner again. Instead of feeling sorry for myself, I decided to use those emotions. I decided that I was going to do something that would prevent this from happening to as many youths as I could. I decided I was going to put action behind my words and follow through. I used those feelings as a motivation that pushed me to create an organization that would be an asset to the entire community. In his death, I found a reason to be a role model, a mentor. He became my reason to take advantage of every opportunity I had as a chance to change someone else's life! Paris Wicks II became a part of my reason.

Another major turning point in my life came shortly after Paris passed away. I was riding in the car with my son whom by this time was eleven years old. Riding in the car is one of the best places to talk to your child. It's quiet, one on one and you're not looking at each other, so it's less intimidating for a child. Needless to say, whenever we are in the car, I am in full blown lecture mode. On that particular day, I was talking to him about the importance of education, how he was expected to graduate from high school and move on to college. I was telling him about the importance of having a degree and increasing his opportunities.

One phrase from him sent my life in a different direction! He suddenly stopped, gave me eye contact and said "Dad, why didn't you graduate from college?" Of course, I was speechless! Once I recovered from being caught off guard, I was honest with him. I told him how I pretty much partied my way through two years and flunked out. I told him that I went to prison before I had the chance to go back and finish. At that moment I realized that as parents we could sit and preach to our kids all day long. We can chastise them, lecture them and tell them all the right things to do in life. But our words are nothing compared to the actions we take to be the example. Our actions are what they see and what they will remember most! Not what Dad said, but what Dad did!

After all of my lectures about the importance of his education, having to explain to him why I didn't have one left me with a sickening feeling in my stomach. Right then, I decided that I was going to make sure that was the last time he would ever have to ask me that! The example I wanted to set for my son gave me the power of another reason for me to improve myself. A week later I re-enrolled at Youngstown State University just in time to start the new semester! At that point, I had been out of school for fifteen years! I didn't know what I was going to major in. I didn't know how I was going to manage to go to school and to work. But I was positive of one thing; I was getting a degree! For ten months I woke up at six am and drove an hour to school. When the school day was over, I went to work in the evenings. By the end of the year, I had achieved a 3.6-grade point average! The highest grade point average I had ever secured in my life! I made the Dean's list both semesters! My self-confidence soared! I was able to be in good standing academically allowing me to transfer to a college closer to home. Two years later I was able to walk that stage and receive my degree!Present at my graduation were my mother, son and brother. Those are the people that I chose to spend that moment with. My mother, the one who never judged me or turned her back on me. Through thick and thin she was the one that I knew loved me unconditionally. My brother. So much potential, I wanted him there as motivation that we could be better! He is now in his second year of college! My son, my inspiration. My reason.

Right now ask yourself what your reason is. What motivates you, what pushes you and what drives you? In other words, what is your reason to succeed, overcome or to exist? I can guarantee you that if you're sitting there right now and you cannot specifically point out what your reason is, odds are you are not where you want to be in life! A person who does not have a reason will never find it necessary to improve their life. No matter how great this motivational book your reading is, a person without reason will remain unmotivated. If you are like I was and stuck in that victim mentality, then you're definitively going to have to find that reason! Whether that reason is a person or people you care about, God or your personal higher power, even if that reason is to prove people wrong...whatever that reason is, find it!

Your reason will make you get up and get back in the fight! Your reason will drive and inspires you! When you're worn out, and you think you just cannot go any harder or take any more punches, your reason will keep you from quitting! When you have realized the power of your reason, you will acquire the courage to take risks needed to get ahead. You will remain internally motivated when all the odds are against you allowing you to push towards a new and more rewarding life!

"He who has a why can endure any how."

Chapter Three

Be Grateful for the Knockdowns and Losses

Each day I am grateful for the opportunity to wake up and breathe another air of life. I am extremely grateful for my health, my family, friends, and career. When the sun awakens me from my sleep every morning, I am grateful for having another opportunity to live out my dreams. I am also grateful for anyone that bought and is reading this book! Ironically, I am also grateful for the knockdowns and losses that have been a part of living here in time and space. Yes! In my battle to win in life, I am grateful for all the knockdowns and losses I have endured!

How is it possible to be grateful for those times when life caught us with a devastating punch leaving us reeling against the ropes or even down for the count? No one could be that unbelievably positive right? I think that everyone would agree that a life filled with only fortune and sunshine is something most of us dream about. Only if D.J Khalid's "All We Do is Win" could become our reality! Nonetheless desirable, a life free of loses and misfortune is simply not possible. For all the magnificent highs there are lows. For all of our achievements, there are failures. In contrast to all the wonders of life that we experience, there is death. However, if we can be grateful for the moments in which life was the hardest, the moments when we suffered the most, we gain the ability to learn, mature and become stronger human beings as we maneuver our way through life.

During the first of my many trips to the great state of Florida, I can recall driving down I95 with the widows down and experiencing the most magnificent rays of sunshine that I had ever seen or felt. As I drove, I marveled at the scenery, the lush vegetation, the beautiful palm trees and the miles of beaches that lined the coast. For someone born and raised in Ohio, this view was astonishing! Add to the fact that I had spent the most of the last decade in prison; it became even more beautiful. In the middle of my moment, I was suddenly assaulted by a rainstorm so powerful that I was forced to pull off the highway! Again, I'm from Ohio where snow blizzards are nothing more than a common occurrence. I had never been forced to pull over in an Ohio snow storm! But here I was sitting on the side of the highway in South Florida waiting out the storm. I couldn't help but be highly disappointed because this would no doubt put a damper on my trip to South Beach.

As the rain came pummeling down, I started searching for a good radio station to listen to until the storm subsided. Surprisingly as fast as the storm hit, it disappeared! Just forty-five seconds into my roadside intermission the sun reappeared! As I was once again engulfed in the South Florida sunshine, I rolled my window down taking note that the sun was warmer on my skin than I remembered. As I looked around, it seemed like the colors were brighter! I marveled in how good I felt once the sun started shining again. At that moment, I began to understand that the rain was just as responsible for the beauty of the scenery as the very sunshine that shined down upon me at that moment. At that moment I began to think beyond the rain. Were it not for the rain there wouldn't be the beaches, palm trees or ocean front properties. Without the rain, the sun would essentially burn everything in its path. Without rain, there would be no balance. Had I not experienced that rain storm I may not have fully appreciated the sun that reappeared.

Finally, I reached my destination and sat staring out into the Atlantic Ocean alone. I began to look back on my life which caused me to be all the way "in my feelings" to say the least! I laughed, I cried and most of all I found an appreciation for what I had been through. I became grateful for the bad times because they allowed me to fully appreciate the beauty of the moment I found myself in. Imagine, for six years the largest body of water I had been close to was a mud puddle, and there I was staring out at the Atlantic Ocean! For six years the only surface my feet ever came in contact with was concrete, and there I found myself burying my feet in the warm sand! For six years I hadn't seen a flower or a tree, and here I was surrounded by exotic flowers and vegetation I had only seen on TV or in magazines! And yes, after six years of being surrounded by nothing but men, there I was surrounded by some of the most beautiful women from all over the world! I was not mad at that! I think I fell in love forty-seven times just sitting there on the beach!

As I sat there on the beach, I began to study the other people who were going about their day seemingly oblivious to the wonders that surrounded us. I wondered if they felt what I felt. Did they appreciate this environment as much as I did? I realized that for most of them, they had never been where I had been or gone through what I had gone through. Therefore, there was no way they could feel what I felt. I realized that the people who lived there were so accustomed to the surroundings that they no longer realized how fortunate they were to be living in what I considered paradise. The bad times and the losses led me to a point where I had a greater appreciation and understanding of the magnitude of the moment.

Just as the earth needs both sunshine and rain to create balance, the good and bad in your life serve to create a similar balance. Experiencing both enables you to simultaneously grasp two opposing levels of appreciation. For example, I am not pleased that I lost six years of my freedom. But I am tremendously grateful for the internal process that has brought me to a place of healing, happiness, and wholeness. To me, to fully experience the joy of love and pleasant gratitude, I had to be willing to also breathe in the heartache that life included. When I allowed myself to appreciate the pain of those bad times, my ability to feel a deeper more profound universal gratitude was multiplied a thousand times

Not only do our knockdowns and losses give us an appreciation for the good times, but they also serve in our journey of maturation. In this way, life is similar to photography in being we develop from our negatives. These are the moments in our lives when we learn to deal with life's problems. These are the moments when we learn to lean on our spirituality. They are the moments when we develop empathy for others. Without those kinds of experiences, you might have continued life ignorant of the difficulty others face and possibly even feel entitled to your fortuitous situation.

Another key component in reaching the point of gratefulness for the negative that we encounter in life is in recognizing that the bad times aren't a punishment, they are extraordinary opportunities to learn! A loss can never be a total loss if you learn something as a result of it! There was a spiritual leader who once said, "difficulties come at you at the right time to help you grow and move forward by overcoming them," he observed, "the only real tragedy, comes when we suffer without learning the lesson." I'm reminded of the Peanuts comic strip that I would often read growing up. Charlie Brown walks away from Lucy after suffering a defeat at yet another baseball game. "Another ball game lost! Good Grief!" Charlie moans. "I get tired of losing. Everything I do, I lose!" The ever motivating Lucy responded, "Look at it this way Charlie Brown, we learn more from losing than we do from winning." When you suffer those losses, learn from them! Dissect why you lost, figure out what you can do differently the next time.

In those moments when you can embrace it, you'll see these knockdowns and losses as pivotal moments in your mental and emotional evolution. Believe that your knockdowns and losses are leading you to something greater. Use the bad days as motivation. Remember where you have been and how far you have come, and mostly stay focused on where you are headed. Being grateful for the losses you encounter in life is the sign of a new you being born. A new you who is more self-confident and has high self-esteem and one who no longer frowns in disgust. The result will be a new you who instead smiles when remembering the knockdowns and losses instead of regretting them. Soon you will begin to see your present failure as a temporary condition and the same way you gravitated towards failure, you will rebound from it!

"Sometimes you fall because there is something down there
that you're supposed to find"

Chapter Four

Your Inner Circle

I can sum this chapter up by using Proverbs 13:20 for my readers well versed in The Bible, "He that walketh with wise men shall be wise: but a companion of fools shall be destroyed." Simply put, show me who your friends are and I'll show you your future! During your mission to bounce back from life's knockdowns, you are going to be your own biggest threat or your greatest advantage! As the CEO of your life, you alone have the power to make your reality whatever it is you want it to be! However, never forget that whom you surround yourself with along that journey will also play a pivotal role in determining if your able to get up from that knockdown or if you stay down for the count.

Every champion has a great corner! There are no exceptions to this. The concept of having a great corner in life is just as necessary. In you're battle back, you will need people who will encourage you, inspire you and hold you accountable. Therefore, the next step in your comeback journey is to carefully decide who is going to be a friend, who is going to be an associate and who is going to be a part of your inner circle. Think of your inner circle as those people in your corner that are going to do everything they can to see you win! You have your trainer feeding you directions and words of encouragement. You have your cut man who patches up your cuts and swelling so that you can continue to fight. You have your towel and water guy who is waiting to refuel your thirst and get you feeling refreshed for the start of the next round. All these people in your corner working individually and together to make you a champion! When you have fought your way back from those knockdowns and losses, they will be there celebrating you! They will tell everyone that their guy is the champ! Most importantly, when you suffer setbacks or additional losses, they will still be there believing that you will win the next one!

Your inner circle will be an important tool on your path to bouncing back from your knockdown. These are the people you will take most of your advice from and rather good or bad, these are the people's whose habits you will pick up! Therefore, the prerequisite for allowing anyone to become a part of your inner circle should be that they nourish and inspire you. Your inner circle should consist of people who continuously provide fuel that feeds your flame! Filling your inner circle with these quality people should be a goal in itself! Even if the people whom you surround yourself with have goals and dreams that differ from your own, you will end up feeding off their energy, and they will also feed off your energy. Understand, you are the master carpenter of your life! You have the power to create the kind of inner circle that will help to drive you towards achieving all your goals and reach your dreams with ease. None of us were born to simply exist! We were born to excel and reach success in life! Your inner circle will play a major part in that!

One thing I like to do in my spare time is research prominent people who have reached extraordinary levels of success in their lives. I study the Jay-Z's, the P. Diddy's and the LeBron James's. But I also study individuals like Andrew Carnegie, Bill Gates and Barrack Obama. Despite the obvious differences in these people, one similarity that they all seem to have in common is that they have a very small inner circle. These people may have a lot of acquaintances, they may do business with a wide spectrum of people, but only a select few make it into their inner circle. Sometimes that inner circle includes a close friend or two. Very often it is limited to just family members. In contrast to the level of celerity and notoriety that these people have garnered, their true inner circle consists of people behind the scenes who are rarely seen by those on the outside. Studying these people who have reached the level of success I aspire to reach has allowed me to understand the wisdom of that approach.

To reach success you must limit who can impact your life with their behavior and opinions! You need look no further than Jesus Himself as an example! Even Jesus had an inner circle; he wasn't friends with everybody! He had twelve disciples and He was closer to some than others! To understand the importance of choosing your inner circle wisely look no further than Judas who was a part of His inner circle! If you fail to choose your inner circle wisely, soon you will be dealing with unnecessary frustration, drama, betrayal and other situations that are not conducive to growth and progress. You may even end up being the one who is sacrificed for the good of these so-called friends.

Through experience, I have come to realize the majority of people that you come across in life excel at being critical. At every corner there is someone waiting to criticize your every move. Even when you are successful they find ways to diminish your accomplishments. However, the people in the world who are capable of paying a compliment are few and far between. The fact of the matter is that it takes a great deal of maturity to be happy about the success of others. It takes wisdom not to feel threatened by the talents of others. And it takes humbleness to be willing to learn from the people who are further along in their journey towards success than you are. Not everyone has those gifts. On your comeback journey, it is imperative that you limit your inner circle to people who are encouragers leaving no room for the critical masses.

You should be thinking about the people you surround yourself with and whether or not they deserve to be a part of your inner circle. You can solve this dilemma by observing their actions toward you as the friendship grows deeper. Pay attention; people will expose themselves the closer you become. Some people will begin to feel like it is OK to say whatever they want to you and to treat you any way that they want. The closer you get to them the more they will take advantage of you or disrespect you. Spending time with them will become dependent on what you can do for them or what they can gain. As time passes, the less you will be able to depend on these people. Contrarily, the people who should be in your inner circle, the closer you get to them the more respect they have for you! The better they will treat you, the higher regard they will hold you in. They are those friends who you can call on anytime, and share your deepest challenges.

A major factor in my development and a principle reason as to why my life has become one filled with love, opportunity, motivation and continued progress is due to the people I have surrounded myself with. Outside of my brother Pete and my mother who are the closest people to me, I have my extended family, my inner circle. This is composed of Erica, Shawn, Wayne, and J.R. Though none of us share blood relation, calling them "friends" doesn't nearly justify the magnitude of our relationships. Simply put, Erica is my sister, and the remaining member of my inner circle are my brothers. These people inspire me to be a better person, provide me with the motivation to achieve my goals, empower me to make the changes I need to succeed, and they cheer on my successes! They are each a leader in their own right and live their lives with the same morals and principles that govern my life. They are educated, ambitious and constantly looking for ways to improve themselves and the lives of the people around them. At any given time, someone from my inner circle is starting a business, getting another degree, buying a home, getting married, or publishing a book!

Perhaps my favorite aspect of my inner circle is that we are all individually different with our ways of thinking and seeing the world. It allows the collective to soak up knowledge from different perspectives and provides diversity in the ways that we think. "Iron sharpens iron" as Shawn often perfectly describes our inner circle. The knowledge and experiences we gain individually, ultimately trickles down to the rest of the circle. Picture a bank full of knowledge and experience that you can tap into at your convenience! When I have questions about anything from being a father, business and finances, love or relationships I can call on any number of them. We learn from each other, and we respect each other's opinions. At the end of the day, we know that whatever information we receive is coming from a place of genuine love and a desire to see each other succeed. However, the most valuable characteristic each member of my inner circle possesses is loyalty! I never have to second guess their roles in my life nor question any of their motives! All they want from me is to see me win and to be standing there when the final bell rings celebrating victory! I know that whether I'm on top of the world or down on my luck, their roles in my life will remain the same.

If you look closely at my inner circle, you can see the reflection of each of them in me. You can see the change in the direction of my life that has occurred since they have been in my life. I take parts of Shawn like his business savvy, his leadership qualities, and his dependability. He was just blessed with his first child, my niece, Brooklyn. But way before he had his child, he had already become the God Father of seven! When everyone wants you to be their child's God Father that says a lot about you as a man! When there is a major decision I need to make, most often he's the one I reach out to. I inject parts of Wayne, his maturity and his wisdom. He's the "old man" of the inner circle as we affectionately refer to him as, old school morals and values. As I work to better the lives of at-risk youth in the city, he is my go-to guy for advice. His famous line "Fifth Ave to the Wilbox" describing the inner city neighborhood that he grew up in. The same streets that many of these at-risk youth walk every day. He is the perfect example of "making it out," as he is now a counselor for an alternative school that serves behaviorally challenged students. I also take parts of J.R like his charisma and outgoing demeanor. My guy has the gift of gab, to say the least! But he also has that "je ne sais quoi" that allows him to walk in a room full of a strangers and walk out knowing everyone. It's his gift and what has made him one of the top-selling car salesmen in the state of Ohio for several years running.

Erica," Edub" as I call her is my absolute best friend. We share no relation, but most people assume she is my sister; in fact, we even share the same last name. Erica is one of the closest people in my life. Whether it be a text message, phone call, face-time or in person she is one of two people I speak to every single day, the other being my mother.

Once I graduated from college, I recall telling Erica about my plans to start a youth mentoring program. Before I could get through my whole spill, I looked up and realized she was crying! Not just crying, she had those huge crocodile tears! Once she assured me that she was OK physically, I realized that those tears were not tears of pain or sorrow. Those tears represented her want to see me accomplish my goals and her belief in me! She wanted me to be great! It came from her knowing my struggles and understanding where I wanted to go in life! Not long after that, she gave me the honor of being her son's God Father! What better way to show someone how much you believe in them?

It may surprise you when I say that as far as our personalities, Erica and I are total opposites! She is loud and extremely outgoing, I'm quiet and reserved. She is spontaneous; I like to plan everything out. I may give you a small embrace when I see you, but only if I know you. Whether you're meeting her for the first time or you're a lifelong family member, Erica is going to give you the biggest, most obnoxiously loving hug you have ever experienced in your life...every single time! I use to ask her; why do you have to be so loud? I admit those ridiculous hugs use to get so irritating! My hair would be all messed up and everything! But remember what I said about how people treat you the closer they get to you?

As Erica and I have gotten closer over the years, the things that previously irritated me, became the things I love and appreciate the most about her. They are what make her Erica. As the years have passed, I have had the chance to watch her star in multiple seasons of a web series, perform in musicals and plays, see her on commercials, hear her on the radio and watch her interview celebrities. I realized that a huge personality is part of her gift! I understand why she is loud and outgoing; those are the gifts God gave her to help her reach her destiny. I have no doubt that you will see her on a movie screen soon!

In contrast, before I went to prison, I had three people whom I considered my inner circle. One was unemployed and had eight kids by several different women. One was a hustler/con artist. The last was a drug dealer who dropped out of school in ninth grade. These were my friends, and I say that because they did have love for me. Despite what they did or how they lived their lives, they were who were there for me at that point. But having so much of my time filled with these negative influences no doubt had a direct reflection on the negative path my life had taken.

Looking back on all the time I spent with these people; I cannot recall one positive thing I learned from any of them! When I dropped out of college not one of them said, "Hey! You need to go back to school!" I had no one in my inner circle that slightly suggested that I do anything positive with my life. I believed that because these people were struggling in life just as much as I was, that made them good friends. That made us be able to relate! I believed that because I had known these people so long, I owed them some type of loyalty. Eliminating these people was not something that I enjoyed, but on this elevator of life sometimes you have to stop and let some people off. They had to go!

During your comeback journey, those negative relationships will need to be replaced with a positive one. Those people I left behind, I wish them well, and I do not harbor any ill feelings towards them whatsoever. But there was a time I came in my journey towards winning that I truly I did not fit in with those people anymore. I realized that these people were willing to settle for average and the more I began to strive above that level of mediocrity the more there became conflict! They didn't like that I became committed to my dreams because it reminded them that they were not chasing theirs. One of the biggest reasons people don't follow through with their dream life is fear that they will be left out if they achieve it. Most people give up not because they can't make it, not because they aren't capable but because they are surrounded by people who have settled. People who don't want to see you succeed because that will remind them that they didn't! That is why everyone doesn't deserve to be around you! You have to defend your light with your life. You must surround yourself with people who inspire you! The word inspire comes from the Latin meaning to "breath life into." If you look at your inner circle and don't get inspired then you don't have a circle, you have a cage!

As you read this, consider who you have in your inner circle. Are they the right people? Are they individuals who are going to help you achieve your purpose on earth or are they going to undermine you? Look who you have surrounded yourself with. Are those people throwing logs on your fire or are they constantly raining on it? You have an uncertain amount of time in which to accomplish God's purpose for your life. It is important that you use that time wisely. So be careful of who you allow to be part of your inner circle. And then make sure that you are a good inner circle member to those who you hold most dear!

"Your inner circle are people who understand your past, believe in your future, and accepts you just the way you are."

Chapter Five

Create a Blueprint for Your Future.

You were hurt, you were knocked down, and you were counted out! While down on the canvas of life you wondered how you would ever come back from your latest knockdown. For weeks, months or possibly even years, you scrolled through Instagram wishing your life could be like all those people who seem to have it all. The perfect lives, the perfect homes, and the perfect vacations. But you knew you wanted to do better! You were down, but you wanted to bounce back! That's why you spent so much time scouring motivational quotes and memes for the magic "how to" that would suddenly make everything happen for you.

Now, look at you! You have found a way to pick yourself up! You have taken responsibility for the knockout that you suffered in the last fight! Your reason has given you the motivation and fire to get back in the ring and keep fighting, to not be afraid! You have learned from that loss and replaced your old trainers with new ones who motivate, coach and support you! Your self-confidence is at an all-time high! No more time to waste, now it's time to put your game plan together! Your life blueprint!

No champion just walks into the ring swinging wildly and expects to win! From the bell of the first round, you need to know what you want to do and how you're going to do it! The champions have already mapped out every punch and every bob and weave. They dictate the course of the fight with their blueprint for winning.

But, when there is an opening, they are also prepared to seize the opportunity to land their devastating knockout punch!

Just like in the ring, every champion needs a plan for their life. Believe me, if you don't have a plan you're going to be a part of someone else's! Without a plan, many people will just drift along and continually allow life happen to them. Of course, life would be a lot less complicated if there were a blueprint that works for everyone, but that doesn't exist. We all have our own lives, our battles, and our circumstances. What works for me may not work for you and vice versa. Understanding that there is no one universal blueprint for life helps us to create our blueprint. The good thing is there is no particular way that is right or wrong when it comes to creating a blueprint for your life. A blueprint is quite simply composed of "I am here, I want to get there, and this is how I am going to achieve that."

In the early stages of drafting your life blueprint, understand it will not be fun. It takes some time and deep thinking. You will need to do a lot of meditating, soul searching and writing. It is not something that you should expect to complete in an hour or two. There will be a lot of stress involved as well as indecision. At times you will be discouraged when you come face to face with everything you will need to accomplish to get you from point A to point B. As we all are aware, change is not comfortable, and you will be forced to change a lot of aspects of your life in order to accomplish the goals on your blueprint. However, do not be discouraged, you have made it through the hardest part of your bounce back journey, you got up! Now you move forward. Now you go on the offensive!

There are several factors that you should be considering when you are crafting the blueprint for your life. Ask yourself, what do you value most in life? What drives you to accomplish your dreams? What principles, morals, and values do you live by? What is it that you ultimately wish to achieve in your life? A blueprint takes you from just fantasizing to having a formula for thriving! I'm not talking about a blueprint for your day or your week. I'm talking about a blueprint for your future, a plan for your vision of an extraordinary life! Do not sell yourself short while crafting your blueprint! Your blueprint should be the outcome of exactly what you want your life to become, no matter how grand of an imagination you have! Norman Vincent Peale said it best, "Shoot for the moon, even if you miss, you'll land among the stars!"

Once you decide what your final destination is, you should create a series of short term goals set along the way. These intermediate milestones are created by breaking your long-term goals into short term goals. These short term goals then help you know whether or not you are on the right path to reach your destination. Your short term goals should answer questions like what do you want to achieve this year, this month even today. Do not be discouraged if at first, you can only see the big picture! That is fine! Follow it! Along the way, you will find clues that make the picture clearer. It is similar to zooming in on a picture. The closer you get, the more you can see all the small details. Over time you will continue to refine your blueprint. As you grow and learn your values may change, your wants and needs may alter. As you accomplish goals, you will need to replace them with new ones.

When you are clear of your destination and how to get there, you need to execute your plan. To be able to do that you are going to have to focus on your objectives! Without focus, you will spread your effort, energy, and attention too thin ultimately achieving nothing. Be careful, you should be focused but not obsessed! Being focused does not mean that you work twenty-four hours a day seven days a week. It does not mean that you eliminate every other aspect of your life that is not a part of your blueprint. But you will need to develop the proper focus to achieve your mission.

You will also need to be persistent! One thing that you can be certain of is that failure is inevitable on your way to success! If you think Oprah, Barrack Obama or Warren Buffet became the extraordinarily successful people they have become because they never failed you are mistaken. What made them extraordinary is that they failed and never gave up! It's easy to get discouraged in the face of failure and stop before you reach your destination. But what separates the contenders from the champions is the ability to look failure in the eyes and keep moving forward. Think about this, have you ever truly failed at something that you focused on and were persistent in, something that you put one hundred percent of your effort into? If you did, the only thing that left the results as a failure was the fact that you stopped before you succeeded! I come across so many people who have great ideas and great intentions, but they lack the focus and perseverance to complete their mission. They give up before they reach their destination!

Lastly, you must be willing to put in the work! Late in fights that are particulary close you will hear the commentator say something like "Now we will see who really put the roadwork in." This means we will see who put in the critical, hard work and who just did enough to get by. The same is true in life! The time will come when you are in the metaphorical late rounds in your battle to win in life. Please don't believe that simply crafting your blueprint will make your future the reality that you foresee. Everyone wants success but how many people are willing to put in the work? Are you willing to be the one who is up grinding while everyone else is sleep? Are you willing to skip the parties and the night life to stay at home to work on your goals? You will never achieve champagne standards with a beer work ethic. If you are not prepared to put in the work, then prepare yourself to be just another person who dreamed of success but never realized it in reality. As wonderful as you will feel once you create your life's blueprint, it will be useless without energy and action as the foundation of your plans. Your blueprint can help to encourage you and provide you with a path to realizing your dreams, but it cannot do the work for you!

When I began my blueprint, I was very indecisive as to where I wanted my destination to lead me. Would I be most happy reaching financial success and focusing on the steps to reach that? Or should I focus on more meaningful goals that will leave a lasting legacy? Finally, I decided that what would make me most happy would be a combination of both! All the riches in the world would not ultimately give me happiness, but at the same time, I don't know anyone who wants to struggle through life financially. One thing that truly gives me happiness is teaching and improving the lives of the people around me. At the same time, I enjoy having nice things; I enjoy being a provider and I love taking vacations. In the end, it's my blueprint so why can't I have it all? So I began to craft my blueprint designed to create that balance in my life.

I won't bore you with each goal that I hope to achieve along the path to my destination. But in the end, it leads me to be able to live and to authentically experience life as fully as possible and to consistently learn, grown and become all that I can become. Its leads me to a place where I have grown spiritually, where I can love deeply and to give immensely to others to the best of my ability. When I reach my destination, I will have learned to use all the gifts God has bestowed upon me to make the biggest most positive impact on our beautiful planet and universe.

Once you create your blueprint, you will begin to feel less anxious and restless and more grounded and centered. However, crafting your blueprint is not a one-time thing, it's a lifelong process. You will need to review and your blueprint frequently. The frequent review will help keep you on track with your goals and purposes. I like to review my blueprint at least once a month. At times there are unforeseen issues that may require me to change my blueprint. As I achieve goals, I need to establish new ones. It took me months to draft my blueprint for my life. It took a lot of meditating, soul searching and writing which was difficult and draining work. But it was worth it! Once you draft the blueprint for your life, you unlock the mystery of knowing where you want to go in your life and how to get there!

"If you fail to make a plan for your life chances are you will become a part of someone else's."

Chapter Six

Appreciate the Value of Time

At some point in your journey, you will realize that money, cars, homes and all the other monetary enjoyments of life mean nothing to you. At that point in your journey, time will be the one asset that you will wish you possessed more of! Unfortunately, when you reflect on your life, it will be time that you most often abused and failed to take advantage of. I believe the biggest mistake we make in life is foolishly wasting time! By wasted, I mean the time we spend not doing something of beneficial value to ourselves or someone else.

The first mistake many of us make in regards to how we use our time is by assuming we have plenty of it! According to the data base company Statistica, the average human life expectancy is seventy-nine years old. That sounds like enough time for anyone to accomplish whatever it is they want for their lives, right? Maybe not! Take into consideration that the average person spends twenty-eight years of their life sleeping, ten and a half years working and nine years on TV and social media. That leaves us with about thirty years. A lot less than seventy-nine but still a significant amount of time, right? Maybe not! Consider other life activities such as the six years doing chores. The four years we spend eating and drinking. The four years we spend on education. Two and a half years grooming. Two and a half years shopping. For those of us who can do simple subtraction, that leaves us with about ten years, give or take a year. Ten years to accomplish all of our goals and dreams! Not so long now is it? On your journey to bounce back from the knockdown or loss that you have endured, you will need to learn to take advantage of the time that you have.

When people hear my story, they are often shocked by the fact that I did six years in prison. They look at my five foot nine, one hundred sixty found frame and wonder how I survived. One of the first questions I always get is "what was the worst thing about prison?" They assume I'm going to say obvious things like being locked in a cage, being away from my family, the food or not having the comfort of a woman. To put it bluntly, yes all those things sucked! But for me, the absolute worse and scariest thing about prison was the fear of dying while locked behind those barbwire fences! Don't get me wrong; I didn't live in a constant state of paranoia. I wasn't looking over my shoulder, sleeping with one eye open waiting for someone to stab me and dying a violent death. In my six years I never actually saw anyone murdered in prison. But I saw plenty who suffered heart attacks, lost their lives to cancer and other diseases. My fear was not in death itself; my fear lies in the fact that my legacy would end with me being a failure. Could you imagine the last and final sentence on your life is "He died in prison?" Forever to be known by the worse thing, the biggest mistake you've ever made! I couldn't imagine having a son who would have to explain that he never knew his father and why. In retrospect, I appreciate that fear now in my life. That fear has instilled in me the value of taking advantage of every minute I have to re-write my legacy!

I love my life! I love being alive, and I hope I live until I'm one hundred and fifty years old! But I admit, that fear of what my legacy could have been is still lingering inside of me. As much as I love being alive, that feeling still makes me envision my death from time to time. I don't think about how I go; I think about what will be left afterward. Most often, I picture my gravestone and the things they will write on it. I picture the left side of that gravestone where they put the day I was born. I picture the right side of that gravestone which is the day I passed away. Then I picture that area right in between, that dash. It is the most important thing on my headstone. That dash is what my son will remember of me. That dash will represent everything that I did in my life.

More important than when I was born or when I passed away, that dash represents the lives I was able to impact, the mark I was able to leave on this planet and a legacy that can never be altered. That dash says, "yes he got knocked down but boy did he get up!" I live for that dash! That dash pushes me! That dash makes me remember my reason! It puts everything that I've done or wish to do in perspective. People ask me why I work so hard, why I hardly sleep and why I don't have much time to socialize. It's because I have ten years to make that dash the greatest story that can be told! I don't have a minute to waste!

Inside of all our sub consciousness, there lie two conflicting voices. As with any yin and yang confrontation, there is a good and bad side to each of these voices. There is one voice that pushes us to stop being stagnant. It encourages us to go out there and create the life we want instead of letting life happen to us! It rings in our ears like the classic Outkast song "Get Up, Get Out and Get Something," encouraging us not to let the days of our lives pass by! This voice motivates us to take action to achieve goals and work towards a brighter future. This voice wants us to capitalize on our opportunities that come across our paths. This voice is uplifting and supportive! On the opposing spectrum, there is that "other voice."

This voice constricts our potential and squeezes the life out of us like a python wrapping around its prey. This voice makes us lazy, complacent and keeps us stuck in the same state of mind. This voice that says "relax, you have time, just do it tomorrow," is our worse enemy! Every day these two voices are fighting a war over the control of your future! Alas, in any war there is a winner and a loser. In this war, the winner is going to be the voice you listen to the most. The voice that wins will be the voice you feed, the one that you amplify.

Consciously or unconsciously, we make a choice each day of our lives to listen to one of these voices. Which voice are you listening to? Whether you are embracing the poetic beauty of the positive voice or listening to the voice of negativity, that voice will define your story. Either you will take advantage of the time you have to write a positive ever lasting legacy, or you will continue to waste time leaving to chance what your story will be. When you are down and fighting to regain a hold of your life, you must not let the voice of negativity continue to grow increasingly stronger. Far too often we listen to the counterproductive voice that makes us waste time; makes us abuse it! This passiveness when it comes to time leads many of us to display a lack of action. It makes us too comfortable. We quickly lose track of the notion that each minute, hour, day and week that goes by, time continues to grow smaller and smaller.

As I move well into middle age, I hoard my time like an old miser hoards his money. Time has become truly valuable to me and any minute not spent with people or activities I care about feels like time stolen from me. Like most people, when I was young, I thought I was invincible. So, I wasted my time with people who didn't have any real value to me and engaged in activities that didn't do much for my life in the overall scheme of things. Admittedly, this squandered time was due partly to the fact that, when your young, you don't necessarily know what will bring benefit to you long term. But early in life, much like having a healthy bank account, it doesn't seem to matter because at that point, you have plenty of time to spend. Once you reach a certain age and look back on your life, you ponder and perhaps regret the immense opportunity costs of the time you have let go by being unproductive. Soon you realize that time symbolizes the definition of non-renewable resource. By non-renewable, once the time is lost or wasted, you can never get it back! As we so painfully learn, not only is time nonrenewable, it is also irreversible.

One of the most valuable bits of advice I have recently received came in the form of a quote. It said, "never get so busy making a living that you forget to make a life." What I had to learn is taking advantage of your time in this life does not mean that you only spend it working or making a living! It also means appreciating the time you have to live! It means doing the things you like to do. It means creating memories and experiencing new things. It means putting work aside to devote your time to family and love. As Shakespeare said, "Time is very slow for those who want, very fast for those who are scared, very long for those who are sad, and very short for those who celebrate, but for those who love, time is eternal." In your journey towards bouncing back from life's knockdown, you will need to work harder, faster and longer to accomplish your mission. But please, once in a while stop and devote your time to appreciate the wonderful gifts that God has created for us to enjoy. Allow time to devote to love and service for others. Being there for others. That time is precious and certainly does not fall into the category of waste.

You have the power to prevent wasted time, and many of us are doing that. Before we make decisions, before we act, we need to think about how we're spending our time. We need to focus on want we want to accomplish. What makes the heart burn with passion, what wakes you up in the morning, what's your reason? I want to see the transformation of how we use our time. I want to see a change in habit. The appreciation of the time that you're given. I want you to pause the next time you find yourself wasting time on things that damage you, and think about why you've decided to shorten your lifespan. You're killing yourself; it's not a joke! Because you can't recycle the time, you waste. So use your time and make it work for you. Stop killing time, because eventually, that turns around, and it will kill you.

"The only people who dare to waste time are the ones who have failed to discover the value of it."

Chapter Seven

Believe in Yourself

I'm writing this chapter on Christmas Day in Kent, Ohio the city where I was raised for most of my life. I am surrounded by family, enjoying the laughs and smiles as the children open their Christmas gifts. In times like these, I like to reflect on the year and the changes that have occurred during that time. Of course, I am thankful for life, health, family and all the wonderful experiences that life offers us. However, as I ponder on what I'm the most thankful for this year, I've focused on the one thing that has continued to make a substantial difference in my life. I am thankful that I believe in myself!

I just chuckled to myself in retrospect because I am very much aware that the odds say there is no way I should have accomplished the goals that I have. The system is not set up for this! Let's make no bones about it; I am a convicted felon. Ex-Convict. And even after eleven years of being a free man, I am still a "Former inmate." (according to a recent write up in the Akron Beacon Journal). Who told me that I could be a mentor and a role model? What gave me the audacity to believe that I can be an inspiration for others, a blessing to others? I must be crazy to think that I could start not one, not two but three businesses in three years? What made me believe that I could not only publish a book but own my own publishing company? I must have missed the memo! That's not what a black man raised by a single mother in low-income housing is supposed to do! That is not what a "former inmate," is supposed to aspire to!

I must admit, I enjoy this feeling immensely! It's not out of a sense of arrogance; it's because I love being the underdog! I chuckle to myself because, despite my past, I have a confidence that leads me to believe that I can accomplish anything! Not only do I believe it, I expect it! This confidence comes as a result of my experiences, what I have overcome and what I've achieved despite the odds. It is a result of the countless family and friends that have supported me throughout my journey. It is a result of the fire that burns inside of me as a result of my reason. Regardless of the source of my confidence, it is the one quality that allows me to not only talk about what I'm grateful for but also live it out for the world to witness! This quality is having an unwavering belief in myself!

Steal a moment to think about how different your life would be if you possessed absolutely unshakable confidence in your ability to achieve anything? Even as you read this, there are most likely things that come to your mind that you feel you cannot realistically achieve. But, if you were guaranteed to achieve anything you set your mind to, what would you aspire to? What would you dare to dream if your belief in yourself was so intense that you had no fears of failure whatsoever? If this were true, you would shoot for the stars! There would be no limit to the possibilities that your mind could produce! If you are a person who settles for mediocrity, if you don't dream the biggest dreams and desires the most wonderful life you can envision for yourself, it is only because you don't believe in yourself! It has nothing to do with your circumstances, your surroundings, your knockdowns, and losses nor your lack of resources. It is one hundred percent mental! The only way that you can start the process of turning your dream into reality is by believing in yourself.

In my experience, there is one significant difference between people who succeed in life as opposed to those who don't. The difference is not found through intelligence, opportunity or resources. The difference lies in the fact that successful people believe in themselves regardless of their situations! Instead of playing the victim role and coming up with excuses as to why things won't work, they find reasons that it will! Instead of focusing on the resources that they lack, they focus on the resources that they possess and find a way to make it work!

When I began my comeback journey, I developed a set of lofty goals. The majority of people I shared those goals with believed that my past would prevent me from achieving them. Others believed that not only could I not achieve them, they believed no one could! I run into those same people now, and the first thing they say is "I can't believe you did what you said you were going to do!" Ten years ago I would have taken that as them telling me to my face that they thought I was "full of it." Today, it doesn't bother me because I know that we as a culture and society have been conditioned to doubt not only ourselves but those around us. Get used to it! There is always going to be someone that is going to doubt everything you do. They are going to question your sincerity and call in to question your morals. I owe a lot to these pessimistic people because instead of listening to the doubters and allowing that seed of negativity to strip away my confidence, I use it to my advantage. Instead of allowing my past to be a hindrance, I use it as an asset! Who better to mentor, advise and change the direction of an at-risk youth's life better than someone who has been in their shoes? Someone who is not just telling them what he thinks, but what he knows! Someone who has taken the punches, been knocked down and counted out but has fought his way back! Those knockdowns and those losses which represent the worse moments of my life are what qualifies me for the job! Fortunately for myself, I have become one of those people who never allow the doubts of others to put a limit on my possibilities. I am a person who believes that if I continue to move forward, then I will figure it out. As I sit here with my eight-year-old niece who is trying to take my phone, I'm thankful that I am one of these people.

Like most people, I was not born with this level of confidence or belief in myself. There were most certainty times when I had low self-esteem and suffered from that victim mentality. But as a result of my experiences and actions, I have learned to be fearless! Every small accomplishment builds that belief in myself. Each day I take one more step. Each day I try to accomplish one more goal. When you live each day in this way soon, you will start gaining momentum. Once you have momentum, you won't be able to stop, and everything will seem easier to you. Even if things get tough, you won't feel like it's tough because you will have grown more confident. You will make progress and progress will make you happy. Achieving those small to intermediate goals will help you do more and be more. Soon all of this will become second nature to you. Your confidence, your self-esteem and most importantly your belief in yourself will shine through like the champion you were placed on this earth to be! Soon people will want to be like you and look to you for help and advice. You will try to help them and motivate them by giving them the same information that helped you. But they won't turn your words into action because they won't believe in themselves.

Do not be discouraged if your belief in yourself is slow to build! One goal I set for myself was to become a motivational speaker. I wanted to embark on county wide speaking tours and get paid to tell my story! There was only one problem with that; I was always terrible at public speaking! Whenever I would get in front of an audience, my voice would start doing this weird cracking thing, and I would get extremely nervous! I always had this fear that I would forget everything I wanted to say and end up making a fool of myself. Because of this, I put my speaking career on hold for some years!

What made me say "I'm going to go for it" is when I graduated from college. The ideal result desired by most people after walking that stage and receiving a degree is to be able to get a job or qualify for some type of employment. The biggest thing that graduating from college did for me was to make me believe in myself! For most people, finishing college will be one of the hardest things you will ever do. It is a process that tests you not just mentally but physically! It will burn you out and frustrate you at every turn. The pressure in immense! The exams, the assignments, the deadlines! Then you have to deal with financial aid, and scheduling classes. It's a lot! I walked away saying "If I can do this I can do anything!" That accomplished goal fed the belief in myself!

Once I decided I was going to embark on my speaking career, I began sending emails to all the correctional institutions in Ohio. After a few weeks, I received word from Loraine Correctional Institution saying they would like to have me come in and speak to the inmates! I gladly accepted! Not long after we confirmed the date, I started thinking to myself "what did I just do?" My first reaction was to think I "bit off more than I could chew!" But it was too late to turn back now!

For three weeks I rehearsed my speech endlessly. I read it over and over, I said it out loud, I performed in a mirror. I performed it for friends. I recorded myself, so I could hear how I sounded and watched my body language. By the time those three weeks were up, I had mastered my speech and my presentation! Finally, the day came, and I traveled to the prison. As I stood in front of those men and prepared to deliver my very first motivational speech, a total calm came over me. I was different! That nervous, voice cracking guy was gone! The man that delivered his speech do those men that day had no fear whatsoever! From the beginning of my speech to the end I delivered flawlessly! I knew I had killed it! No lie, halfway through my speech I even said to myself "I am killing it!" I knew this was true even more so when I received a standing ovation and signed my very first autographs!

This did not happen because I was suddenly a gifted speaker. I did not become more talented. It didn't happen because my vocabulary increased or because I learned how to stay calm. It happened because I believed in myself! Instead of walking in there doubting myself, I told myself "you got this!" Instead of worrying about forgetting my speech, I told myself "I put in the work, and I would not fail!" I told myself that I had already overcome the hardest part of my journey, this was nothing! This belief in myself allowed me to overcome all my past fears, go out there and be my best me!

What is your dream? Every one of us has dreams, and we know they are achievable because we have seen so many people before turn their dreams into reality. Now, do you believe that you can accomplish your dreams? I know that sounds like a cliché but if you don't believe in yourself no one else will! If you don't believe in yourself now, choose to do so because it's just a matter of choosing.

Choose to believe in yourself and give yourself a chance. Lastly, ask yourself how you would feel and act if your dream was accomplished? You'd feel wonderful right? You deserve to feel like that! You deserve to accomplish everything that your heart desires. And why shouldn't you? Your life is your life. You decide who and what you're going to be by believing in yourself!

Unfortunately, believing in yourself is not a full proof method which guarantees every idea you have will work out the way you plan it. You have to be willing to not only think differently but also to experiment with new ideas and trust that you'll discover a way to make them work. If the first way doesn't work, try a different way of doing it. Believe it is possible. Believe that you can do it regardless of what anyone says or where you are in life. Visualize it. Think about exactly what your life would look like if you had already achieved your dream. Then, always act in a way this is consistent with where you want to go.

Believing in yourself will soon open your eyes to endless possibilities in your life. However, at the beginning of your journey, you may find it difficult. There are going to be people who doubt you and make it hard for you to believe in yourself. Not only will you need to fight through the people around you doubting you, but also you will need to fight through the fact that we've been conditioned throughout our lives to doubt ourselves. Once you begin to rid yourself of these self-doubts, your self-esteem and self-confidence will rise like the champion you are!

Everything that you ever have in life and everything that you can accomplish is the result of your belief in yourself and the belief that it's possible. An important element in this process is remaining true to yourself! Always be true to the very best that is inside you. Each day that you awake and have another shot at winning, make sure you live that day consistent with your highest values and goals. This is the only way you truly learn how to believe in yourself. I strongly plead with you to never compromise your integrity by trying to be someone or something that is not true for you. More importantly, never compromise your potential growth due to doubts that can only limit your reality. Instead, embrace your confidence and believe in yourself because you really can do anything you put your mind to!

"Believe in yourself when nobody else does."

Chapter Eight

A Higher Power

I sought to be very cautious with this final chapter because I want this to be a book that all people, all races, all genders, and all religions can draw inspiration from. I recognize that religion and spirituality are very serious subjects and people throughout the world have spent centuries studying these topics. I am admittedly far from being an expert in the field. Nevertheless, I believe that someone's religion, spirituality or belief in a higher power is their own to decide and no one should feel the right to question that person's choice! No matter what religion you are, no matter what you believe in, I would request that you accept the other person's idea.

In the 1993 motion picture Menace to Society, there was a thought-provoking scene starring Charles Dutton. In the scene, he is having a conversation about religion with his teenage son Shareef and Shareef's friend, Cain. In the scene, Shareef has recently converted to Islam and Cain is questioning Shareef's father about the religion. The father who is a Christian man says, "If Allah makes him a better man than Jesus then I'm all for it!" I feel the same way. Whatever religion you are and whatever you call your God or your higher power, I am all for it if that makes you a better person. I don't believe that any one religion is "right," I believe that the salvation of your soul depends on your own belief that no one can question.

My personal experience with religion was through the influence of my grandparents. My grandfather is a retired Baptist preacher, and my grandmother is a Jehovah's Witness. I know that sounds like an unlikely union, but after nearly seventy years of marriage, I would say they have made it work! As a child, I didn't realize the difference in my grandparent's denominations. All I knew was that grandpa's church was as the kids say now "lit" and grandmas church was not only excruciatingly boring, but they didn't give out presents on Christmas or birthdays because it was against their beliefs. As the years went by, I was able to understand more of the differences between their two denominations. Soon I had to come face to face with the elephant in the room. I had so many questions! Questions like, is there a hell? Should I be praying through Jesus or directly to God? Do I need to be baptized or do I earn my way into heaven by being obedient to God's commands? Which of my grandparents should I side with or believe? Understand, these are the two people whom I respect most in the world! But, if someone is right, then someone has to be wrong. What happens to the person who is wrong? What I wasn't going to do was question either of their faith or beliefs. What it made me do was find my path, find what I believe in.

For a moment think to yourself, what is it that you truly believe in? I'm not talking about what your parents or grandparents taught you to believe in. Not what you learned from a teacher, pastor or watching Sunday morning inspirational programs. I want to know what you believe in, what do you have faith in, what is your higher power? Consider this, take everything someone else has influenced you to believe and hypothetically remove it. If no one told you to be Christian would you be Muslim? If no one told you to be Muslim would you be Jewish? Now tell me what you believe now. One of the scariest things about becoming cognitively aware of your true self is coming to the conclusion that most of your beliefs belong to someone else! To me, that is a sad existence! In actuality, you are living someone else life! Your beliefs, morals, values, and perceptions are all a result of what someone else thinks and feels! Remember, the people who have the hardest time finding comfort and happiness in their lives are the ones who are walking in someone else's footsteps!

Before you can begin to connect to your higher power, you must connect to yourself! Knowing yourself will help you decide exactly what it is that you believe in! I encourage you to do your research! It is OK to listen to other people and to hear other perspectives and other beliefs. But form your own thoughts and opinions as well. Do some meditating and soul searching! When you know yourself, you will be able to relate to your higher power, recognize your gifts and see the path that your higher power wants you to travel. I can admit that my concept of a higher power has changed dozens of times over the years. My willingness to completely turn things over to His will has been a lot easier said than done. I know that my gift and my calling is to connect with people and offer my experiences as motivation to change lives. However, following that calling is rarely the most rewarding financially. In the beginning, there were times when I had to decide if I was going to pay my rent at home or pay the rent at the mentoring center. Complicating things, even more, is the fact that I am a man of many talents and highly educated. Often it was hard to resist the urge to pursue my selfish desires and do something else that would bring more income. But just as His hand guided me out of my darkest moments, my higher power made sure that I was taken care of. I may not have everything I want or could have, but I always receive what I need. When I began to seek my higher power's will for my life, it became more important than my human desires. That's when I was rewarded with abundance! Not in the monetary ways that you may think, but with respect, admiration, appreciation, love, and success. When I finally submitted to His will, my life began to evolve in ways that are nothing short of miraculous!

Still, if you were to ask me right now what my religion or denomination is, I couldn't tell you. What I believe in is something greater than me. I believe in a force that is the controlling factor in everything! Yes, everything! It cannot be created nor can it be destroyed. This higher power assembled the universe and causes the earth to rotate around the sun. It makes the flowers bloom in spring and makes the grass grow. It provides that spark that makes your heart continue to beat without you prompting it to do so. I call this higher power God. You may choose to call him Jesus, Yahweh, Buddha, Jehovah or Allah, whatever is your preference. As I said, I am not an expert in the field of religion, but I believe that all those spiritual beings are one and the same. That higher power is without evil, is good and merciful and will never turn His back on you. If you live by the right principles and live unselfishly, He will provide. When you pray, He will hear you! When you ask for guidance, He will never steer you wrong. Some people will tell me that what I am speaking of is directly in line with the messages from their holy book. The truth is that the primary principles found in all holy books were already profoundly ingrained within all of our hearts. If you believe common sense and knowing right from wrong are exclusive only to your own beliefs, then you need to open yourself up to the rest of the world's beliefs.

I will never tell someone what to believe in. I will never tell someone that they should second guess their beliefs. But what I tell everyone is that you have to believe in something! If you don't believe in God or any of the other spiritual beings I named, believe in miracles! If you don't believe in miracles, then believe in humanity! If you don't believe in humanity, then believe in mercy, compassion, and bravery. It is your choice what you believe in, but promise me you will believe!

Once you strongly identify with a higher power, now you can capitalize by allowing it to help you improve the quality of your life. It's time to let your higher power do His work! It starts with awareness. Understanding that your own life was created by this higher power gives you the ability to tap into that energy. It gives you the ability to take advantage of the gifts God has instilled in you. You connect to these gifts through the creative process. As humans, we are all born with amazing creativity! You and I can conceive an idea! That may seem like the simplest of scenarios. But in all actuality, it is evidence of how we've been created in the likeness of our higher power's energy. The consciousness of your spiritual energy is essential. Think about it; you encapsulate a bit of "God's" power when you create an image in your mind. This creative energy has the potential to elevate your life from mediocre to magnificent; you only have to allow it. The process begins with you and your awareness of your higher power's existence. Allow your creativity to flow!

Now you have a choice! Now that you are connected to your higher power choose the path to abundance. Allow yourself to dream and envision the life that you not only want but the life you deserve! Your higher power wants that for you! Remember back in chapter one where we realized the power of taking responsibility? It is now your responsibility to harness this energy and aim it in the proper direction. You are not only a spiritual being, but you also have intellect. Human beings are not like the birds and the flowers, which must naturally follow God's order. We have the ability to choose to follow the Godly order of abundance and creativity.

Believe it or not, you don't have all the answers. What is even harder to believe is that I don't have all the answers! Obviously, I'm working on my next career as a comedian. Seriously, it's perfectly fine to surrender to what you don't know because your brain is not always your ally. This creates less dependence on self and more on divine inspiration. I can recall the times when I would pray and pray for an answer to life's problems. I would wait for a sign, for a beacon to spring from the sky and say "here is your answer!" What I failed to realize is that my higher power was in all things, all people! When I opened myself up to the people around me, I began to find those answers. I truly believe that God has purposely placed those individuals in my life. So when you find yourself in doubt or indecision, communicate it with the people around you, your inner circle. Getting feedback from others pulls your higher power in. So, don't believe everything you think, when you share with others you're in reality letting a higher power in.

From this point onward move as if you have no excuses! You are created by a Higher Power, and made in that likeness, so do not let your situation convince you otherwise! You must believe that you are meant for joyful and abundant living! Remember, you have the ability because you have in you a spark of the energy that is the source of everything! It is up to you to recognize it, choose it, and use it to create the life you desire! The choice is yours!

"There is trust in there being a spirit who loves me and wants me to have love in my life. I trust this higher power; it is what keeps me moving forward no matter what happens."

But We Get Up...Bouncing Back After Life's Knockdowns

By A.T. Wright

The following are a series of short stories that I have read in my journey that have provided me added motivation during some of my most trying times. I hope that you can also find inspiration.

The Elephant Rope

One day a gentleman was walking through a camp where they kept a herd of Elephants. As he was watching the elephants, he realized that the only thing holding the elephants back from escaping the camp was a small rope tied around each of one of their ankles. There were no cages or chains used anywhere in the camp!

As the man gazed upon the elephants, he was completely confused as to why the elephants didn't just use their strength to break the small ropes around their ankles and escape. They easily could do it but yet none of them even tried.

Curious and wanting to know the answer, he asked the trainer nearby why the elephants were just standing there and never tried to escape.

The trainer replied "when they were young and much smaller we use the same size rope to tie them and at that age its strong enough to hold them. As they grow up, they are conditioned to believe they cannot break away. They believe the rope can hold them, so they never try to break it. The only reason the elephants weren't breaking away and escaping is because over time they adopted the belief that it just wasn't possible.

Moral of the story. No matter how much the world tries to hold you back, always continue with the belief that what, you want to achieve is possible. Believing you can become successful is the most important step in actually achieving it.

The Lesson of the Butterfly

A man spent days watching a butterfly struggling to emerge from its cocoon. One day a small opening appeared. He sat and watched the butterfly for several hours as it struggled to force its body through the tiny little hole until suddenly, it stopped making any progress at all. To the man, it appeared like the butterfly was stuck. So the man decided to help the butterfly. He took a pair of scissors and snipped off the remaining bit of the cocoon. The butterfly then emerged easily, although it had a swollen body and small, shriveled wings.

The man didn't think anything of it and sat there waiting for hours for the wings to enlarge to support the butterfly. But that never happened. The butterfly spent the rest of its life unable to fly crawling around with the tiny wings and a swollen body.

Despite the kind heart of the man, he didn't understand that the restricting cocoon and the struggle needed by the butterfly to get itself out of the small opening were God's way of forcing fluid from the body of the butterfly into its wings to prepare itself for flying once it was out of the cocoon.

Moral of the story: Just like the butterfly, our struggles in life develop our strengths. Without struggles, we never grow and never get stronger, so it's important for us to tackle challenges on our own, not by relying on others.

Shark Bait

During a research experiment, marine biologists placed a shark into a large water tank and then released several small fish into the tank. As you would expect, the shark had a feeding frenzy! He swam around and eventually devoured all of the smaller fish.

The marine biologist then inserted a strong piece of clear fiberglass into the tank, creating two separate partitions. She then put the shark on one side of the fiberglass and a new set of fish on the other side. Again, the shark attacked, but this time instead of getting to the fish he was slammed into the fiberglass and bounced off. Undeterred, the shark kept repeating this behavior every few minutes to no avail. Meanwhile, the fish swam around unharmed on the other side.

Eventually, the shark gave up about an hour into the experiment.

This experiment was repeated several times over the next few weeks. Each time the shark got less aggressive and made fewer attempts to attack the bait fish until eventually, the shark got tired of hitting the fiberglass divider and simply stopped attacking altogether.

The marine biologists then removed the fiberglass divider, but the shark didn't attack. The shark was trained now to believe a barrier existed between him and the fish, so the fish swam wherever they wished free from harm.

Moral of the story: Many of us after experiencing setbacks and failures, emotionally give up and stop trying. Like the shark in the tank, we believe that because we have failed in the past, we will always fail. In other words, we continue to see a barrier in our heads, even when there is no barrier there between where we are and where we want to go.

Potatoes, Eggs, and Coffee.

A girl was telling her father one day that her life was so miserable and she didn't know how she was going to make it. She was tired of fighting and struggling all the time. It seemed like every time she solved one problem another popped up to replace it.

Her father, a chef, took her to the kitchen. He filled three pots with water and placed each on a high fire. Once the three pots began to boil, he placed potatoes in one pot, eggs in another pot and ground coffee in the third pot.

He then let them sit and boil without saying anything to the daughter. The daughter, moaned and groaned and impatiently waited to wondering what he was doing. After twenty minutes, he turned the fire off on the pots. He placed the potatoes in a bowl. He took the eggs out and placed them in a bowl. Then he took the coffee and placed it in a cup.

He asked his daughter what do you see? Potatoes, eggs, and coffee she said. Look closer he said, and touch the potatoes. She did and noted that they were soft. He then asked her to take an egg and break it. After pulling off the shell, she observed that the egg was hard-boiled now. Finally, he told her to take a sip of the coffee, and its rich aroma brought a smile to her face.

Father, what does this mean she asked. He then explained that the potatoes, the eggs, and the coffee beans had each faced the same adversity- the boiling water. However, each one reacted differently. The potato went in strong, hard and unrelenting. But in boiling water it became soft. The egg was fragile, with a thin outer shell protecting its liquid interior until it was put in the boiling water.

Then the inside of the egg became hard. However, the ground coffee beans were unique. After they were exposed to the boiling water, they changed the water and created something new.

Which are you he asked his daughter, when adversity knocks on your door, how do you respond? Are you a potato, an egg or a coffee bean?

Moral of the story: In life, things will happen to us and around us, but the only thing that truly matters is what happens within us.

Ms. Lucille Wright

When my world went crazy, you never let go.

When the ground became shaky, you gave me hope.

You helped me see the power in me.

At my worse and my best,

you've loved

Unconditionally

In Loving Memory of

Shavon Wright, Veral Hardesty, Sandra Hardesty, Hazel Hardesty-Younger, Norma Sales, Carol Mims, Roger D. Boykin, Malcolm Wright, Paris Wicks II

But We Get Up 2!

Coming November 2019

www.ingramcontent.com/pod-product-compliance
Lightning Source LLC
Chambersburg PA
CBHW060658030426
42337CB00017B/2679